10/06

Tongue Twisters

A Buddy Book
by **U.R. Phunny**

Buddy **BOOKS**

More Jokes!

Published by ABDO Publishing Company, 4940 Viking Drive, Suite 622, Edina, Minnesota 55435.
Copyright © 2005 by Abdo Consulting Group, Inc. International copyrights reserved in all countries. No part of this book may be reproduced in any form without written permission from the publisher.

Printed in the United States.

Edited by: Sarah Tieck
Contributing Editors: Jeff Lorge, Michael P. Goecke
Graphic Design: Deborah Coldiron
Illustrations by: Deborah Coldiron and Maria Hosley

Library of Congress Cataloging-in-Publication Data

Phunny, U.R., 1970-
  Tongue Twisters / U.R. Phunny.
      p. cm. — (More jokes!)
  Includes index.
  ISBN 1-59197-877-7
    1. Tongue twisters. I. Title. II. Series.

PN6371.5.P498 2005
818'.602—dc22

2004055446

Susie's sister sipped seven
sodas swiftly.

Veronica visited very vicious volcanoes.

Gloria's glittery glasses glow.

Tall Tom took tiny Tim to Texas.

Freddie's friend Fran fries frogs.

A skunk sat on a stump.
The stump thought
the skunk stunk.
The skunk thought
the stump stunk.
What stunk?
The skunk or the stump?

Purple paper people,
purple paper people,
purple paper people.

Sparky's special spaceship
speeded into spectacular space.

Lucky Louie liked licking
lollipops lazily.

Double bubble gum
bubbles double.

Fat frogs flying past fast.

Betty's brother, Billy,
blew bubbles badly.

Gertie's great-grandma grew
aghast at Gertie's grammar.

Brenda's brother, Brad, brought
Brenda bread for breakfast.

Crisp crusts crackle crunchily.

Baboon bamboo,
baboon bamboo,
baboon bamboo,
baboon bamboo,
baboon bamboo,
baboon bamboo.

You've no need to light
a night-light,
on a light night like tonight,
for a night-light's
light is a slight light,
and tonight's a night that's light.

When a night's light,
like tonight's light,
it is really not quite right
to light night-lights with
their slight lights
on a light night like tonight.

Which witch wished which wicked wish?

The sixth sick sheik's sixth sheep's sick.

Silly Sally swiftly shooed
seven silly sheep.
The seven silly sheep
Silly Sally shooed
shilly-shallied south.

Craig crocodile crawled 'cross
crooked crawling creepies.

Zany Zelda zapped Zeke's zebra.

Jolly juggling jesters jauntily
juggled jingling jacks.

A sailor went to sea to see
what he could see.
And all he could see
was sea, sea, sea.

The owner of an inside inn
was inside his inside inn with his
in-laws outside his inside inn.

Ben buys black bananas
by the bunch.

Three free throws.

Sleepy Slick slipped
on a slimy, slippery sled.

Sly Sam slurps Sally's soup.

Drew dreamed a dreadful
dragon dropped Drew's drum.

Freshly fried flying fish.

Six slippery snails slid
slowly seaward.

I saw a saw that could outsaw
any other saw I ever saw.

If you tell Tom to tell
a tongue twister,
his tongue will be twisted,
as tongue twisters twist tongues.

A stegosaurus stepped on
Steven's stepsister.

If Stu chews shoes,
should Stu choose
the shoes he chews?

The doctoring doctor
doctors the doctor
the way the doctoring doctor
wants to doctor the doctor.
Not the way the doctored doctor
wants to be doctored.

Selfish shellfish.

Claire's class clapped for the clumsy clown.

These sheep shouldn't
sleep in a shack,
sheep should sleep in a shed.

Any noise annoys an oyster,
but a noisy noise
annoys an oyster more.

Yippy yanked young
Yolanda's yucky yellow yo-yo.

We surely shall see the
sun shine soon.

A two-toed tree toad
loved a three-toed she-toad
who lived up in a tree.

The two-toed tree toad
tried to win the three-toed
she-toad's heart.
But the two-toed
tree toad tried in vain.
He couldn't please her whim.

From her tree toad bower,
with her three-toed power,
the three-toed
she-toad vetoed him.

Web Sites

Visit ABDO Publishing Company on the World Wide Web. Joke Web sites for children are featured on our Book Links page. These links are monitored and updated to provide the silliest information available.

www.abdopub.com